Easter Experiences

liturgies and sketches for Holy Week

by Susan M Brown

Scottish
Christian PRESS

First published in Great Britain
in 2004 by Scottish Christian Press
21 Young Street, Edinburgh EH2 4HU

Performing and Copying:

these books are designed to provide resources mainly for churches and
amateur groups that want to use drama in worship, study and mission.
**You are free to perform any of these plays and sketches and do
not need permission, but we would appreciate receiving news of
any productions. Our plays are protected by copyright and so we
ask that you buy copies for each actor when you purchase one.**
We hope that you will find them useful for the work of the Kingdom.

Contact us for further information at:
enquiry@scottishchristianpress.org.uk

ISBN 1904325130
D.L.: SE-4413-2004 in Spain

Cover illustration by Iain Campbell. Typeset by Heather Macpherson

Produced in the UK by Bookchase
Printed in Spain

Introduction

Holy Week has become an increasingly important time for me in my faith-life. I find it the perfect 'excuse' to spend time walking through the events that led up to Jesus' death and resurrection. Through reflection on what is the pivotal point of the Christian faith, I find my awareness of my own place in those events increased; and I find too a heightened sense of the horror of all Jesus was willing to go through in order to break the power of death and separation for the likes of me.

Because it is such an important time for me personally, I like to encourage others to consider making the same discovery, in the hope that they too might experience the full impact of Easter. The stories themselves speak powerfully of the loving, one hundred percent commitment of God to his people. They do so in such a way that they have no great need for further theological expansion or elucidation - their message is so painfully and beautifully clear.

There are two sets of sketches presented here, one uses eyewitness accounts from the point of view of a court scenario (where the congregation is invited to play the part of the jury), the other uses a series of monologues again from eyewitnesses. They are set in the week leading up to Jesus' crucifixion. The sketches can stand alone as an alternative for the usual Holy Week services, but using the suggested prayers and meditation for each day they provide the basis for ten contemplative and challenging liturgies.

I know there are those who feel that church once a week is commitment enough, but these services invite congregations to come together daily between Palm Sunday and Good Friday, so that Easter Sunday becomes all the more meaningful. The complete services are relatively short acts of worship (Monday through Maundy Thursday) and can be held at lunchtime, in the early evening, or both (whichever best suits your church or community). Since it has a history and attracts more interest, the slightly fuller Good Friday sessions are probably more appropriately conducted in the evening.

As the *Easter Experiences* are less formal than a traditional Sunday act of worship, a more informal setting is appropriate. In Dornoch cathedral, we move seats into the crossing and conduct them there, moving back to the pews for the longer Good Friday service. *Easter Experiences* would work equally well in a hall or a classroom. Quiet music is played on a CD before and after; we also play (on CD again) the Taizé chant: 'Jesus Remember Me', referred to in the following pages.

Various members of the congregation take on the roles of the characters. These people should be chosen because their age, sex and vocal ability are appropriate to the words they are being asked to speak. The impact of *Easter Experiences* hinges on how well these people convey their stories, so it is important to choose them carefully and let them read through the script in advance. All the readings are done script in hand and need not be learned by heart.

In the first set, the rest of the congregation become involved as 'jurors' and it is good if the Lawyer is able to walk among them - he/she will be posing questions with the script on a clipboard. Each of those called to the witness stand should have a stand to go to! The lectern can be used, if there is one, or a raised dais of some sort. In the second set, the congregation is invited to listen to the eyewitness' monologues, so no special seating is required. The chairs for the congregation should be arranged in such a way that all can see and it is easy for the characters to enter and leave.

The orders of service provide a very brief summary of events and serve as a reminder to those present (and those unable to attend) of what has happened earlier in the week. (Inevitably there will be those who cannot make it to all the services). Each day's proceedings can stand on its own and should therefore make sense, even if people have missed one or two.

As is traditional, the Good Friday services end without a Benediction to give a stark reminder of the awfulness of the day. Please be aware that in the first set of sketches, the scene finishes with the door slamming - this can cause alarm, but also has a finality that is as chilling as the events of the day itself.

The final section contains the dawn service for Easter Sunday, and the Easter Sunday evening service (Emmaus). We intend you to use these after both sets of Holy Week sketches. (I have found that those who have walked through the Easter Experience during the week enjoy the sunrise service on the beach, followed by breakfast together in the church hall). We round off our Easter festivities with an evening celebration of Holy Communion Emmaus style - where the congregation is invited to walk with the two disciples into the crossing. Then, in one very large circle, they are invited to share the bread and the wine and meet in those elements the reality of the risen Christ. Again, this service is intended to follow both sets of sketches.

I hope all this preamble has not detracted from the simplicity of what these scripts and services are trying to do - to make Easter a personal experience. Use and enjoy them. Allow them both to upset and cheer you. And then go on to meet the risen Christ.

Contents

Cast List, Props and Music Resources

Cast list for court scenario (characters and time needed)

Lawyer (Monday through Friday)
Reader (Monday through Friday)
Benjamin Ben Jacob, a salesman (Monday)
Mary Magdalene (Tuesday)
A Pharisee (Wednesday)
Peter (Thursday and Friday)
Pontius Pilate (Friday)
Mary, the Mother of Jesus (Friday)
Officer of the Guard (Friday)

Props
A witness stand: your church lectern, a raised platform (dais)
A clipboard (for the Lawyer)
Note the nearest available door for slamming (or use a recording)

Costumes
No costumes, per se. A simple black gown, however, may be appropriate for the Lawyer to wear.

Layout
The congregation should be seated in such a way that the Lawyer can walk easily among them; they are members of the jury.

Technical requirements
CD player for music before and after the sketches. It may be possible to feed this through your sound system, otherwise choose a player appropriate to the size of your performance space.

Lighting: be creative with what you have!

Cast for eyewitness' monologues

(characters and time needed):
Woman, housewife (Monday)
Woman visitor (Tuesday)
Peter (Wednesday)
Landlord (Thursday)
Peter/ Woman/ Carpenter/ Official
Mary (mother of Jesus) (Friday)

Props

Pint of beer (for Peter), coffee and tea (for the female characters) preferably pourable from a recognisable pot or flask, a hip flask (for the Official). Bar stool, table and chair as required.

Costumes

Not necessary, ordinary clothing will do.

Layout

Whatever is convenient - perhaps chairs in a semicircle, or in rows - as appropriate to your locality.

Technical information

CD player for music during the services. It may be possible to feed this through your sound system, otherwise choose a player appropriate to the size of your performance space.

Lighting: be creative with what you have!

Easter Sunday Dawn Service

Cast

Mary Magdalen

Easter Sunday Emmaus (evening) Service

Characters

Cleopas
One other disciple

Music and Other Resources

Hymns and songs are taken from *Songs of God's People* (SOGP) and the *Church Hymnary, 3rd edition (CH3)* with the appropriate number reference.

Jesus Remember Me is a song written by Jacques Berthier of the Taizé community.

A full list of Taizé songs and prayers may be found at www.taize.fr

Recordings of Taizé music available in the UK from Alliance Music include: Songs of Taizé vols 1&2 artist: the St Thomas Music Group, ID no's 2-1901592 and 2-1901892.

Deep Still - Authentic Celtic Hymns and Songs of Praise (suggested for use in the Monologues Good Friday service) is a CD available from Christian bookshops. The song *Lamb of God* is by Keri-Ann Rostad.

Holy Week Courtroom Scenario

Monday:

Leader   Let us pray:

Lord Jesus Christ,
Grant us the courage to walk with you over these next few days.
Open our senses to feel your anguish,
to taste your fear,
to smell the hatred and the suspicion ...
to touch your shattered body ...
and to glimpse the hope you never let go.
May we learn how to love,
how to give,
and, from watching you,
may our lives be changed for ever.
You are already close, draw us from the shadows we try to hide in and lift our faces to look into yours.
It is in your name and for your sake that we ask this, our Lord Jesus Christ.
Amen.

Lawyer   Why?
Why did things change so dramatically in the space of just a few days?
Why did the crowds, who so noisily and happily welcomed Jesus into Jerusalem just yesterday, end up turning on him asking for him to be put to death - in fact demanding that he should be?
What happened?

Throughout the course of this Holy Week we will invite onto the witness stand some of those who played a part in the

5

events that unfolded. You are asked as jurors in this case to listen carefully to the stories being told and to reflect prayerfully upon the evidence given.

The information you will receive is information based on Scripture. There is no law against discussing the details of the case outside these four walls and in fact, as jurors, you are encouraged so to do.

Reader	*(From Matthew 21:12-13)* And Jesus entered the Temple of God and drove out all who bought and sold in the Temple, and he overturned the tables of the money-changers and the seats of those who sold pigeons. He said to them, 'It is written, "My house shall be called a house of prayer"; but you make it a den of robbers.'
Lawyer	I call upon our first witness, Mr Benjamin Ben Jacob. *(Calls of 'Benjamin Ben Jacob'. He enters and takes the witness stand.)* Mr Ben Jacob, am I right in saying that you are a stallholder in the central Temple precincts?
Benjamin	I am.
Lawyer	How long have you worked there?
Benjamin	Since I was a child - it was my father's stall and ever since I could walk I've sat there with him.

Lawyer	You have many years' experience then, of selling pigeons?
Benjamin	And of changing money.
Lawyer	Changing money?
Benjamin	Certainly. The people who come to the Temple, especially during the Passover celebrations, come from all over the country. They bring their own coins and we're able to change them into the local currency.
Lawyer	For a fee?
Benjamin	Of course! Business is business - we have to charge for our services. It's what they expect! It's how we live!
Lawyer	Then what happens?
Benjamin	Once they have the proper currency they can then buy the birds or the animals they need for offering to God.
Lawyer	And these birds and animals ...
Benjamin	They buy from me - or from any of the other stallholders. But we have an excellent reputation for having the finest produce, and we have an agreement with the priests.
Lawyer	An agreement with the priests - what sort of agreement?

Benjamin	Well, as you know, every animal being offered has to get the priests' approval - only the best will do for God. If the priests know that the animal comes from our stall ... they pass it - no problem - because they know it's the best.
Lawyer	None of your animals has ever been rejected by the priests?
Benjamin	Not in my lifetime! We have an agreement - Ben Jacob's birds are the finest!
Lawyer	Ladies and gentlemen, I ask you to note that Mr Ben Jacob here, sells the very best of produce - he has an agreement with the priests which means any animals bought from him are automatically accepted ... But why? He is a businessman. He changes people's money, people who have travelled miles to get to the Temple, and he does so, naturally, at a price ... Does that price include, I wonder, not only his own exchange fee, but a fee to buy off the priests ...?
Benjamin	(angrily) Now wait a minute ...
Lawyer	Mr Ben Jacob, you charge people for exchanging their money and you charge them for buying your birds?
Benjamin	Yes, but so does ...
Lawyer	Thank you. Can I turn your thoughts now to the matter in hand? To the question of what happened on a Monday pretty much like this when you were at your stall.

Benjamin	You mean the Monday *he* came?
Lawyer	If you mean by '*he*' the defendant known at the time as Jesus of Nazareth, then yes - the Monday '*he*' came.
Benjamin	It was terrible. There we were doing as we usually do ...
Lawyer	Buying and selling.
Benjamin	Buying and selling - when out of the blue he came tearing in.
Lawyer	Jesus, you mean.
Benjamin	Yes, him. He came in and in an absolute rage started turning over all our tables and chairs. The coins spilled onto the floor. The birds and the animals started squawking - the noise was unbelievable!
Lawyer	Did he give any reason for his anger?
Benjamin	He just kept shouting that his father's house was supposed to be a house of prayer and that it seemed to have become a den of thieves!
Lawyer	Had he been drinking?
Benjamin	No, I don't think so.

Lawyer	Was he known as someone with mental health problems?
Benjamin	Not to my knowledge. He'd been in the Temple quite a few times before and usually just sat down to teach people. This time though, he seemed to explode... He even used a whip on us!
Lawyer	A whip?
Benjamin	He made it out of cords - and boy did it sting. We had to run to escape him.
Lawyer	You were hit by him?
Benjamin	Well ... almost - if I hadn't moved as quickly as I had, I would have been.
Lawyer	Ladies and gentlemen, want you to note that according to Mr Ben Jacob, this attack was quite unprovoked. No prior warning was given and those in the Temple precincts suffered both verbal and possibly physical abuse at the hands of the accused. Can I ask you Mr Ben Jacob; was this behaviour unusual in your eyes for Jesus?
Benjamin	I told you already, he usually just came in and sat down. He had quite a following of people who seemed to enjoy his style of teaching. The sorts of people you don't usually see in and around the Temple ... I haven't heard of him causing any trouble anywhere else - not trouble like this - he did upset folk though - especially the likes of the Scribes and the Pharisees. They make no bones about how much he annoys

them - they say he constantly flouts the law, thinks he's above it…

Lawyer   Thank you Mr Ben Jacob. Ladies and gentlemen of the jury, I give you your first witness. A witness who admits he's out to make a profit but who reckons the attack he and others were subjected to in the Temple was quite unjustified. Mr Ben Jacob, please step down.

(Exit Benjamin)

Lawyer   I give you a moment to consider now what you've heard before you retire for the night …

(leaves)

(The service continues. Play 'Jesus, Remember Me'- Taizé Chant - very quietly. After it has played three times speak over the music)

Leader   *Jesus, remember us …*
As guilty as the stallholders of self-righteous indignation and of blindness to our own faults

Jesus, remember us …
So quick to stand on our own dignity - and so slow to defend the dignity of others …

Jesus, remember us …
Not always able to see you in new things … wary of change and of what you might ask us …

Jesus, remember us ...
Fearful of reaching out to really grasp the hope that you offer

Jesus, please remember us when you come into your kingdom

(Benediction) *Now go, to think again of what you have heard, open to*
hearing more ...
And may the blessing of God Almighty, Father, Son and Holy
Spirit be with you all this night and for ever more. Amen.

Tuesday:

Leader   Let us pray:

Lord Jesus Christ,
as we journey with you from the streets of Jerusalem,
to the Temple courtyards,
to people's homes and the upper room,
and eventually out of the city to that terrible hill,
amaze us again with the depth of your commitment to those
around you ...
to us ... and to all people - even in the face of your own
despair ...
With you as our teacher and our example, make us as
sensitive and selfless as you.
This we ask in your name and for your sake.
Amen.

Lawyer   Throughout the course of this Holy Week we're inviting onto
the witness stand some of those who played a part in the
events of the first Easter. You are asked, as the jurors in this
case, to listen carefully to the stories being told and to reflect
prayerfully upon the evidence given.

The information you will receive is information based on
Scripture. There is no law against discussing any of the
details outside these four walls and in fact, as jurors, you are
encouraged so to do.

So far we have heard from one irate stallholder - the case
continues ...

Reader   *(From Mark 14:3-9)*
While Jesus was in Bethany, reclining at the table in the
home of a man known as Simon the Leper, a woman came
with an alabaster jar of very expensive perfume, made of

13

pure nard. She broke the jar and poured the perfume on his head.

Some of those present were saying indignantly to one another, 'Why this waste of perfume? It could have been sold for more than a year's wages and the money given to the poor.' And they rebuked her harshly.

'Leave her alone,' said Jesus, 'Why are you bothering her? She has done a beautiful thing to me. The poor you will always have with you, and you can help them any time you want. But you will not always have me. She did what she could. She poured perfume on my body beforehand to prepare for my burial. I tell you the truth, wherever the gospel is preached throughout the world, what she has done will also be told in memory of her.'

Lawyer   I call upon our second witness, Mary Magdala.

              (Calls of 'Mary Magdala'. She enters and takes
                        the witness stand.)

            Miss, or is it Mrs Magdala?

Mary   Most people just call me Mary.

Lawyer   Mary - can I ask you what you do for a living?

Mary   You can, but I'm not sure it's relevant.

Lawyer   I'm just trying to establish, for the ladies and gentlemen of
            the jury, what kind of a reputation you have.

Mary	If you mean with the authorities, then probably lower than the low. I'm … er, well, let's just say I'm not their type.
Lawyer	Not their type?
Mary	Oh, don't get me wrong, I believe and everything, especially now, but I'm not the usual kind of church-going girl.
Lawyer	What do you mean you believe especially now?
Mary	Since I met him, I mean.
Lawyer	Him being …?
Mary	Jesus. Jesus of Nazareth. He has changed my life. Given me hope. Helped me find faith and a new sense of dignity.
Lawyer	Miss, I mean Mary, can I take you back to one particular occasion when you met Jesus? To the time you met him in the house of Simon the leper.
Mary	I remember it so vividly - as though it was just yesterday. Jesus had been invited for a meal. There was something so sad about him. Something so … so … just looking at him filled me with tears.
Lawyer	Was he upset that night?

Mary	Not on the surface. Not so that you could see - at least Simon didn't seem to notice anything strange about him. I don't know what it was - I couldn't put my finger on it - just call it feminine intuition - but I felt something was wrong and I wanted to do something about it. So I went home to get the perfume and I poured it over him because, somehow, it just seemed the right thing to do.
Lawyer	You took a whole jar of perfume and poured it over him?
Mary	The whole jar.
Lawyer	Was this a run-of-the-mill perfume - an every day one?
Mary	No.
Lawyer	It was an expensive perfume, then?
Mary	Yes.
Lawyer	Very expensive?
Mary	Very!
Lawyer	And you used the whole jar?
Mary	Yes. The whole jar.

Lawyer	Ladies and gentlemen I want you to note that this woman spared no expense on Jesus. Mary, can I ask you why? Are you so rich you can afford such extravagance?
Mary	I'm not rich, no - and to be honest I'm not sure why I did it - other than because I wanted to ...
Lawyer	Was he happy with what you did? Jesus, I mean.
Mary	He didn't object. I think, like me, he felt he needed it.
Lawyer	But I thought Jesus was a man of the people. Out to help the poor and the pushed aside - could that perfume not have been sold and the money used to help those he was supposed to care so much about?
Mary	That's what Judas said - always a man for the money that one - but sometimes people need more than money.
Lawyer	And Jesus needed more than money?
Mary	Yes! He needed to know someone cared - and he needed to have more than words alone telling him that.
Lawyer	So it didn't bother him that the cost of the perfume you poured over him could have fed three, or perhaps even four, needy families for a month?

Mary	The perfume wasn't his - it was mine. I chose to do what I did with it and given the chance I'd do it over again! He needed its gentleness, its sweetness - yes, even its luxury... I don't regret my actions for a minute - and I don't think he does either!
Lawyer	Ladies and gentleman, you've heard this woman in her own words tell you that she thinks Jesus wanted her to use the perfume on him. You've heard too what the money, if the perfume had been sold, could have bought. You've also heard about the air of sadness that seemed to be surrounding Jesus - although there is however, no tangible evidence to back this up - just feminine intuition.

Mary, can I ask you to stand down?

(Exit Mary)

Ladies and gentlemen of the jury, please take the time again this evening, before retiring for the night to be re-called to appear again tomorrow, to consider in quietness the evidence you have heard...

(leaves)

(The service continues. Play 'Jesus, Remember Me'. After it has played three times, speak over the music...)

| Leader | *Jesus, remember us ...*
our reluctance to give you any more than we have to ...

Jesus, remember us ...
The fuss we make of what's not important ... our reluctance to do what is ... |
|---|---|

Jesus, remember us ...
Our slowness to consider your feelings ... and our demands
that you consider ours ...

Jesus, remember us ...
Fill us with a desire to worship you with the whole of our
being ... and not to hold back ...

Jesus, please remember us when you come into your
kingdom.

(Benediction)   *Take what you have heard with you ... sense the truth behind*
the words;
and as you go may the blessing of God Almighty, the love of
his Son and the peace of his Spirit stay with you this night
and always ...
Amen.

Wednesday:

Leader   Let us pray:

Lord Jesus Christ, even in the midst of your journey to the cross you thought of others.
You were sensitive to their pain, to their fears and, although your own load was unbearably heavy, you never expected anyone else to carry more than they could bear …
You, who gave your all, understood when others held back - although you longed for them not to …
And you in your anguish comforted them in their discomfort. Even now, as we meet here, you meet with us to help and to heal …
give us the grace to let you …
and give us too the grace to respond to your love with love. In your name and for your sake we ask this.
Amen.

Lawyer   Throughout the course of this Holy Week we're inviting onto the witness stand some of those who played a part in the events of the first Easter. You are asked as jurors to listen carefully to the stories being told and to reflect prayerfully upon the evidence given.

The information you will receive is information based on Scripture. There is no law against discussing any of the details outside these four walls and in fact, as jurors, you are encouraged so to do.

So far we have heard from one irate stallholder and from a very moved Mary Magdala … our trial continues …

Reader   *(From Matthew 26:1-5)*
When Jesus had finished all these sayings, he said to his disciples, 'You know that after two days the Passover is

coming, and the Son of Man will be delivered up to be crucified.'

Then the chief priests and the elders of the people gathered in the palace of the High Priest Caiaphas, and took counsel together in order to arrest Jesus by stealth ... and kill him. But they said, 'Not during the feast, lest there be a tumult of the people.'

Lawyer   Tonight we hear more evidence from those involved in the events of what we now call Holy Week. We will hear from the principal party for the prosecution - the Pharisees. Who is to speak on their behalf?

                        (Pharisee enter)

Pharisee   I will.

Lawyer   Please take the stand.

                        (Pharisee takes the witness stand)

            You are a Pharisee, then?

Pharisee   I am.

Lawyer   And for the benefit of the jurors, can you please explain what a Pharisee is?

Pharisee   There are some who interpret the word Pharisee as meaning 'separated one'- and that probably says a lot about us. In the main we're not priests, we're just ordinary Jews who like to stick strictly to the letter of the law - and just to make absolutely certain we do stick to it, we make a few extra rules for ourselves - to build a fence round the law if you like, to lessen the danger of us doing what we shouldn't.

Lawyer   So, for you, the laws guiding your faith are important?

Pharisee   Extremely important - nothing more so.

Lawyer   If a fellow Jew were to bend those rules a little, or even break the law, how would you view such a course of action?

Pharisee   I would condemn them. God's laws are meant to be kept - strictly kept.

Lawyer   But surely you don't expect everyone to be able to aspire to the high demands and standards you, as Pharisees, set yourselves?

Pharisee   I admit it takes a lot of effort and determination.

Lawyer   And not everyone is able to put in that effort and determination?

Pharisee   Not everyone has the inclination to put in the effort.

Lawyer   So, you're special?

Pharisee   If being willing to give God his rightful place makes me special, then yes, I'm special.

Lawyer	'If being willing to give God his rightful place makes me special, then yes, I'm special.' Ladies and gentlemen of the jury, please note how puffed up ...
Pharisee	Really! These are your words, not mine!
Lawyer	No, Sir, on the contrary they're your words - I simply repeated them. 'Not everyone has the inclination to give God his place.' ... For a man like you, to whom the practice of your faith is so important, seeing others flout God's laws must be upsetting.
Pharisee	It's upsetting because it means they have no real regard for God.
Lawyer	And you do.
Pharisee	To me, he is everything.
Lawyer	Do their actions ever make you angry?
Pharisee	Not angry for myself ... but angry, yes, for God.
Lawyer	As a Pharisee you are, are you not, fairly used to sitting in judgement over those who fail to keep the law?
Pharisee	If you're asking if I play my part in helping to police the laws of my faith, then yes, I do.

Lawyer	And who are those whom you, as Pharisees, are inclined to deal with most harshly?
Pharisee	Those who deliberately and openly break the rules of the faith and encourage others to do the same.
Lawyer	Perhaps they heal on the Sabbath? In the Temple? In full view of all the worshippers gathered there - making it look as though such actions are acceptable?
Pharisee	Exactly!
Lawyer	Or perhaps they encourage their hungry friends to eat an ear of corn on the Sabbath, as they walk through the fields?
Pharisee	Precisely! The Sabbath is quite clearly set out to be a day of rest - no work is allowed and picking an ear of corn - although it seems harmless enough - is the thin end of the wedge. If everyone picked an ear, then soon whole fields could be harvested on the Sabbath.
Lawyer	But what if the person has a good excuse?
Pharisee	There can be no excuse for breaking the law.
Lawyer	What if the sick couldn't stand even just one more day of pain? What if the hungry should faint for want of just one ear of corn?

Pharisee	The law is the law and that's that.
Lawyer	Ladies and gentlemen, 'The law is the law'. There is nothing more important. Those who break it deserve to be rejected, to be punished!
Pharisee	Well, we can't have every Tom, Dick or Benjamin who comes rampaging through the Temple or the countryside making up his own rules as he goes along - it just won't do!
Lawyer	Tell me, as a Pharisee, what does Scripture say about the coming Messiah?
Pharisee	Oh, don't start on that one! Do you know how many people a year claim to be the Messiah?
Lawyer	But look at the Scriptures …
Pharisee	And every one of those crazy claimants has at least a Scripture or two to back up their argument!
Lawyer	So Jesus of Nazareth is just another?
Pharisee	He's just another - believe me, he's just another. More dangerous than most though.
Lawyer	Why more dangerous?

Pharisee	Because he managed to convince so many that there was something special about him - oh, he's a clever one, that one! Performing healing tricks, evading all our questions, bringing in all sorts of undesirables …
Lawyer	Undesirables?
Pharisee	People you wouldn't normally see in the Temple from one year's end to the next! He brings them in off the street, not in the least bit concerned about how unclean they are and how they might defile the rest of us …
Lawyer	Would I be correct in saying that Jesus, more than most, provoked the ire of Pharisees?
Pharisee	He provoked it to perfection!
Lawyer	Thank you for your honesty, sir! Can I ask you to stand down?
Pharisee	His sort just can't be tolerated - not by those who are truly God's people …
Lawyer	Thank you, please stand down.

(Exit Pharisee)

Ladies and gentlemen, you have heard from one man - one out of a significant and influential group of men - ready to admit that they've got to the stage where even the mere mention of the name Jesus causes their blood pressure to rise. To them, he is blatantly heretical. He flouts the law - thinks himself above it, this is what our witness suggests ... And so he must be dealt with ...

I want you to remember this testimony, to think of its implications, and to do that quietly before you retire for the night. The jury to be re-called tomorrow ... (leaves)

(The service continues. Play 'Jesus, Remember Me'. After it has played three times, speak over the music ...)

Leader   *Jesus, remember us ...*
           The ones who find it easier to stick to the letter of the law
           rather than the spirit ...

           Jesus, remember us ...
           So quick to condemn ... so slow to welcome and accept ...

           Jesus, remember us ...
           So wary of those who are different ... who offer different
           thoughts ... ask for different actions ...

           Jesus, remember us ...
           So quick to see the splinter in another's eye ... so slow to see
           the plank in our own ...

           Jesus, please remember us when you come into your kingdom

(Benediction)   *Go now to be open to new ways, new thoughts, new habits,*
           knowing that the God who is the same yesterday, today and
           forever
           is also new every morning and walks with you into every new
           opportunity.
           May his blessing, the blessing of Father, Son and Holy Spirit,
           be with you all,
           now and always ...
           Amen.

Thursday:

Leader   Let us pray:

*Lord Jesus Christ, you knew what lay in store for you and still
you went ahead.*
You shared a meal with your friends;
*you took their feet in your hands, washed them and dried
between their toes ...*
*and you did all that knowing that they would desert you just
when you needed them most ...*
and never once did you blame them.
*To be able to show such grace in the midst of your own
suffering is mind-blowing,*
it's beyond our understanding ...
and still you forgive ... even us.
*To you, our gracious Lord, be all praise and all glory now
and for evermore.*
Amen.

Lawyer   Throughout the course of this Holy Week we're inviting onto
the witness stand some of those who played a part in the
events of the first Easter. You are asked, as the jurors in this
case, to listen carefully to the stories being told and to reflect
prayerfully upon the evidence given.

The information you will receive is information based on
Scripture. There is no law against discussing any of the
details outside these four walls and in fact, as jurors, you are
encouraged so to do.

So far we have heard from one irate stallholder, from a very
moved Mary Magdala and from a highly indignant Pharisee
... our trial continues.

Reader	*(From John 13:1-5)* Now before the feast of the Passover, when Jesus knew that his hour had come (...) during supper, when the devil had already put it into the heart of Judas Iscariot, Simon's son, to betray him, Jesus rose from supper, laid aside his garments, and girded himself with a towel. Then he poured water into a basin, and began to wash the disciples' feet, and to wipe them with the towel with which he was girded ... *(We continue the story with Mark's version 14:22-25)* (Then) as they were eating, he took bread and blessed and broke it, and gave it to them saying, 'Take, eat: this is my body.' And he took a cup, sand when he had given thanks he gave it to them, and they all drank of it. And he said to them 'This is my blood of the covenant, which is poured out for many. Truly I say to you, I shall not drink again of the fruit of the vine until that day when I drink it new in the kingdom of God.'
Lawyer	If time and financial constraints would allow, we would have each of Jesus' followers taking the witness stand tonight - especially those who were closest to him, those he saw as his disciples. It has, however, been agreed that since we have taken evidence from only the one stallholder and the one Pharisee who spoke for all the others, it is only fair that one disciple should be elected to speak for all the rest. The court felt that it might be difficult to choose who should be invited to speak - but in fact there was, immediately, one eager volunteer. Peter, can I ask you to take the witness stand please? *(Peter takes the witness stand)* Peter, you are a fisherman by trade, are you not?

Peter	I am.
Lawyer	Can you tell the ladies and gentleman of the jury how you, an ordinary fisherman, decided to give up the boats to follow Jesus?
Peter	Well ... he ...
Lawyer	Did you always have a kind of religious bent?
Peter	Well ... I ...
Lawyer	What led you to become a disciple of Jesus of Nazareth?
Peter	If you'd give me the chance, I'd tell you! The short version is we heard him teach ...
Lawyer	We?
Peter	My brother Andrew and I. We heard him teach. He saw us working at our nets and asked if we'd follow him, become fishers of men was how he put it, and we said yes ... and we did.
Lawyer	And you haven't looked back since?
Peter	I wouldn't put it quite like that ... but we certainly don't regret it.

Lawyer	How long were you with him?
Peter	Three years.
Lawyer	Long enough?
Peter	Not at all. I'd have followed him to the ends of the earth and back again - no problem!
Lawyer	You were devoted to him?
Peter	Absolutely!
Lawyer	Absolutely?
Peter	Absolutely!
Lawyer	So devoted to him that when things started to go wrong you disappeared into the shadows … told waitresses and passers-by that you'd never met the man in your life before?

(Silence)

	Peter? Did you hear me?
Peter	I heard you.
Lawyer	So, what happened?

Peter	When?
Lawyer	You had supper together - for Passover.
Peter	The room was made ready for us - everything we needed was there and we were all looking forward to having a great night eating and talking together - celebrating.
Lawyer	Jesus was perfectly happy.
Peter	Of course he was! He was with us - his friends … except …
Lawyer	Except?
Peter	Well, it's a bit embarrassing to have to admit it, but he did have to give us a bit of a ticking off that night.
Lawyer	'Us' being?
Peter	The twelve of us - his disciples. We'd got into a bit of an argument about who should sit where when we got to heaven and Jesus, while we argued, took off his clothes, wrapped a towel around his middle and began to wash our feet.
Lawyer	He washed your feet?

Peter	Well, we were so busy arguing that none of us was prepared to do what we thought was such a menial task. We were each on our own high horse - and he brought us down again with a thump! Our Master, prepared to be our servant!
Lawyer	How did you all react to such a practical and pointed lesson?
Peter	To be honest I felt so bad that when he came to me I refused to let him wash my feet. 'Don't', I said, but he said if he didn't wash my feet then I wasn't with him ...
Lawyer	So he washed them?
Peter	He washed them.
Lawyer	Ladies and gentlemen of the jury; this man who is accused by the Pharisees and by the stallholders of utter arrogance, got down on his hands and knees and washed the feet of those who were supposed to be serving him.
Peter	Ever so gently and carefully - even drying between our toes
Lawyer	Peter, did things end there? With the foot-washing?
Peter	No, there was more to come. Much more. It's only looking back though, that we got the full significance of what happened - at the time, all you could really say was that there was a kind of strangeness about him ... as though he wasn't really looking forward to things - not as much as we were ...

Lawyer	Go on.

Peter	He was a bit quiet. Talked about his death - as he was prone to do anyway - but that particular night he took some bread and some wine - just the ordinary stuff we had on the table and asked us to use them to remember his body and his blood, which he was giving for us …

Lawyer	He had a premonition, do you think, of what was about to happen? Or did he always have a tendency to look on the bleak side?

Peter	It was more than a premonition … it was as though he knew what lay ahead …

Lawyer	And yet he still went on?

Peter	He still went on.

Lawyer	Have you any idea why, Peter?

(Silence)

Peter … have you any idea why? Why would he willingly walk into a trap he could so easily have escaped from?

Peter	Because he wanted to. He had to. He knew it was the only way to save the rest of us.

Lawyer	You're saying he did this for all of us, Peter?

Peter	I am …

| Lawyer | Peter, I'm going to ask you to stand down now in the full expectation that you will be re-called to the witness stand when we reconvene tomorrow night. Thank you for your answers so far. |

(Exit Peter)

Ladies and gentlemen, you have heard the words of Peter, words backed no doubt, by the other disciples. Jesus, the man the stallholders accused of being angry and wild … the man the Pharisees called 'a rabble-rouser' and 'rebel', the man who praised a woman for pouring expensive perfume over him, took a towel and wrapped it round himself to teach his friends a lesson in humility and then asked them to share ordinary bread and wine as a way of remembering him …
I want you to reflect on the evidence, to pause for a while and think of all you've heard, knowing that you will be re-called here tomorrow to make a decision …

(leaves)

(The service continues. Play 'Jesus, Remember Me'. After it has played three times, speak over the music …)

Leader	*Jesus, remember us … When we become so preoccupied with our own stories that we fail to hear those of others …*
	Jesus, remember us … When we fail to let you love us as you really want to love us …
	Jesus, remember us … When we fail to grasp the message you want us to hear …

35

Jesus, remember us ... When we fail you and let you down ...
when we hurt and disown you ...

Jesus, please remember us, when we come into your kingdom

(Benediction) *Go now, thinking of the enormous strength in apparent*
weakness ...
Amen.

Good Friday:

(NB - this service is longer than the others and should perhaps take place in the evening rather than at lunchtime).

Leader   Let us pray:

Lord Jesus Christ, we cannot even begin to understand why you should have done what you did -
we are filled with shame that you should have had to and with awe that you should want to -
your unselfish love and courage goes beyond anything we have ever seen or known.
We are grateful though, that you did face that terrible cross, and that you did it bearing each one of us in mind.
Open our hearts to you this night, Lord, and open our lives to your Spirit ...
Give us the courage to acknowledge what you did - and our part in it. These prayers we offer in your own name and for your sake.
Amen.

Part One

Lawyer   So far in this case against Jesus, we have heard from a Temple stallholder upset at having, in his words, been threatened both physically and verbally by Jesus whilst going about his lawful business. He claimed Jesus wrecked his stall by turning it over, sending money and animals flying in all directions.

We have heard, too, from a woman who, as a direct result of coming into contact with Jesus, claims to have found new faith and a new way of life ... and who rather extravagantly poured a very expensive jar of perfume over him.

Then we heard the evidence of one of the great and good, the evidence of one of the Pharisees, who, on his own admission, was upset at Jesus' alleged disregard for the laws of his faith and who felt strongly that people like Jesus should be dealt with severely.

And last night it was Peter - one of Jesus' closest friends - who took the stand. He made it clear that he firmly believes that Jesus journeyed to Jerusalem knowing full well what lay in store for him and he claims he did so because he cared far more for other people than he did for himself.

Tonight we continue hearing evidence and take up where we left off, with the events in the upper room ...

I re-call Peter to the witness stand.

(Calls of 'Peter'. He enters and takes the witness stand.)

Peter, you have already told us about the foot washing your Master did and about his taking the bread and wine from the table and sharing it as his body and blood - which sounds, how should I put this, just a little on the morbid side. Was Jesus, in your experience, prone to fits of depression?

Peter   The very opposite - five minutes in his company and usually you felt great ... He was the sort of person who really lifted your spirits ... He wasn't the depressive type at all.

Lawyer   But that night he talked about his death?

Peter   He did - but then he would, wouldn't he? If he knew what was coming.

38

Lawyer	You think he knew what was coming?
Peter	Yes, I think he did.
Lawyer	But how would he have known? Did you or any of the rest of your friends in the room that night, have the same sense of foreboding?
Peter	To be honest we thought he was down because we'd all been arguing again ...
Lawyer	You told us yesterday that you had been arguing about which one of you was the greatest.
Peter	Yes - and I think most of us just assumed he was disappointed with us - we knew we'd made a mess of things again.
Lawyer	But you know now there was more to it than just disappointment about an argument?
Peter	Now we know. And it explains why he got so upset with us again later.
Lawyer	He got upset again?
Peter	After the meal was finished. We'd all gone outside for a bit and as usual Jesus wanted to spend some time in prayer ... He asked us to stay where we were while he went just a little way off. Three times he came back to us and three times he had to wake us up.

Lawyer	But that's hardly surprising - you'd just had a heavy meal - complete with wine, it's hard to stay awake in those circumstances.
Peter	That's what we said - but it didn't cut any ice. And I can understand why - he was obviously going through the mill and none of us appeared to care.
Lawyer	Going through the mill? I thought you'd said he'd gone off just to pray?
Peter	He had. But he was obviously having some crisis of faith or facing some kind of inner turmoil because it was clear to all of us when he came back that he'd been crying - and the sweat was pouring off him.
Lawyer	And you say you're sure he didn't suffer from any mental health problems?
Peter	No, he didn't.
Lawyer	So ... why was he so upset? Just because you couldn't keep awake?
Peter	He was upset because he'd an idea of what was coming.
Lawyer	Which was?
Peter	His arrest. We were out in the garden and out of nowhere this whole batch of armed soldiers appeared - with our brother Judas at the head - and they took him away.

Lawyer	Ladies and gentlemen, I want you to note that it was one of his own followers that handed him over ...
Peter	I'm sad to say it was. The rest of us just stood there - in complete and utter disbelief!
Lawyer	And how does that leave you feeling now?
Peter	I know we shouldn't speak ill of the dead - but if he wasn't dead already I might be sorely tempted to ...
Lawyer	You'd leap to Jesus' defence and knock Judas to the ground?
Peter	I'd do far more than just knock him to the ground!
Lawyer	You'd teach him a thing or two?
Peter	A lesson he'd never forget!
Lawyer	His actions made you angry?
Peter	Furious.
Lawyer	And you're a man, as everyone knows, who acts on impulse - so what did you actually do?

(Silence)

	Peter, I asked you a question, did I not? What did you do to defend Jesus at the time?
Peter	Nothing.
Lawyer	Nothing?
Peter	Nothing.
Lawyer	Neither you nor any of the other disciples made any attempt to help Jesus out?
Peter	No ...
Lawyer	Ladies and gentlemen, none of his closest friends, not one, moved to Jesus' aid. Not one. Why not, Peter? Wasn't he worth it? Did you think so little of him?
Peter	I don't know ... I ... I have no excuse - none.
Lawyer	You just froze ... temporarily?
Peter	Three times, I did it. Three times I denied I'd ever known him. Not once, not twice, but three times ... I swore I'd never known him!
Lawyer	Thank you, Peter ... you may step down.

Peter	I wish I could turn back the clock … You've no idea how much I wish things could have been different …

Lawyer	Thank you Peter, take a seat.

(Exit Peter.)

Ladies and gentlemen of the jury - in the early stages of the evening in question, Jesus washed his friends' feet … he ate with them and made some significant statements about love and about service. Then he went out to pray - and as he did so he showed all the signs of being a man in anguish - his friends, though, took no great notice. In the garden, while at prayer he was arrested. Betrayed, it seems, by one of his own … and quickly abandoned by all the rest.

(Exit Lawyer during hymn)

Hymn	When I survey the wondrous cross (CH3 254)

Part Two

Lawyer	I'd like now to take you on to the next chapter of this tale. It would have been useful at this point, to have been able to bring you Judas as a witness but, for obvious reasons, I cannot. I ask you simply to note that perhaps his death is an indication of the measure of regret he experienced at doing what he did …

Instead … I call upon Pontius Pilate.

(Calls of 'Pontius Pilate'. He enters and takes the witness stand)

Forgive me, Sir, but how should I address you?

Pilate	'Sir' will do.

Lawyer	Sir, you are the Roman Governor in these parts, is that correct?

Pilate	I am.

Lawyer	And as such you are authorised, amongst other things, to convict and even to condemn to death?

Pilate	I am.

Lawyer	Are there any matters of law upon which it is not competent for you to rule?

Pilate	Matters of the faith are usually dealt with by the relevant spiritual authorities - I have no spiritual jurisdiction.

Lawyer	You have no spiritual jurisdiction?

Pilate	None.

Lawyer	But what of the man they call Jesus of Nazareth - did you not rule in his case?

Pilate	I did - but only because the religious authorities did not have the necessary powers to deal with the man as they felt he should be dealt with.

Lawyer	And that means?
Pilate	It means they had, under their own laws, already tried and found him guilty of blasphemy of the highest order. They simply wanted me to sanction the appropriate sentence.
Lawyer	Which was …?
Pilate	The one sentence they could not themselves mete out. Death.
Lawyer	Death?
Pilate	As I said - death! The religious authorities cannot sanction such a sentence, they have to come to me - and sometimes a man of my position has to bow to duty no matter how much it might go against the grain …
Lawyer	Are you suggesting that you didn't want to pass the death sentence?
Pilate	Look - at this time of the year, just as a goodwill gesture, we usually release a prisoner and I suggested that Jesus should be that prisoner since, by the time he came to me, he had already been roughed up. They seemed to have been spitting on him, striking him with whatever was to hand … I thought their thirst for blood might have been satisfied - but they wouldn't have any of it. They wanted him dead and nothing else would do.

Lawyer	They?

| Pilate | The authorities, the crowds, everyone! They chose another prisoner for me to set free - 'Give us Barabbas!' they shouted - what shall I do with Jesus, I asked them? And they shouted again - this time louder 'Crucify him! Crucify him!' And to make matters even worse Jesus refused to defend himself - not a word would he speak - how could I help a man who wouldn't help himself? |

| Lawyer | He wouldn't help himself? |

| Pilate | No! |

| Lawyer | Why would he keep silent, do you think? Was it because he wanted to die? |

| Pilate | I have no idea how these religious guys' minds work. Perhaps martyrdom appealed to him. |

| Lawyer | Could it not be that he realised there was no point in speaking? If, as you said - they wanted him dead and nothing else would do? |

| Pilate | I suppose so ... but then he'd have to have been one incredibly brave man to sit back and take that! |

| Lawyer | One incredibly brave... or foolish man, perhaps? Sir, thank you for taking the time to join us tonight. Please, step down. |

(Exit Pontius Pilate)

Ladies and gentlemen, you have heard the words of Pilate. In his opinion, and he is a man of great experience in these matters, there was no real reason for passing the death sentence other than to keep the peace - it was a way of diffusing a potentially volatile situation. And the death of one man a relatively small price to pray ...

(End)

Hymn   Were you there when they crucified my Lord? (SOGP 114)

Part Three

Lawyer   I call upon Mary, the mother of Jesus, to take the witness stand.

(Calls of 'Mary'. She enters and takes the witness stand)

Mary, I realise how hard it must be for you to be asked to think back to the events of that first Good Friday, but can you tell me, in your own words, what happened that day.

Mary   They made him carry his cross. They all had to - the three of them.

Lawyer	Three?
Mary	Jesus and the two convicted of other crimes. We followed behind. I often wonder if their mothers were there too? I remember, at the time, thinking, hoping that it was all some terrible nightmare, some horrible dream and I'd wake up and everything would be fine again ... but it wasn't ... I wanted to hold him, to tell him everything would be okay - but it wasn't okay ...
Lawyer	Mary, I know this isn't easy for you, but was there something different about Jesus? I know to every good and decent parent their child is special - but was there something more to Jesus?
Mary	*(nodding)* Right from the start. I know you're probably going to find this hard to believe but he was, and still is, God's child - not mine and Joseph's.
Lawyer	So, he's not your son then?
Mary	He is, yes ... and he isn't.
Lawyer	You're not sure if he's yours ...?
Mary	He's God's and he's mine.
Lawyer	That seems to be stretching the bounds of belief a bit but perhaps it might go some way to explaining why Jesus seems to have had an idea of what lay ahead for him - did you see things turning out the way they did?

Mary	Not at all.

Lawyer	You said he was, and is, God's Son ... do you think this is what God wanted? To see him crucified?

Mary	I've been asking myself that question over and over again. I can't believe any parent would want to see their child die ... and certainly not a parent who loves that child as deeply as God does ...

Lawyer	So you're saying that this can't be what God intended - it wasn't part of his plan? He lost control of the situation?

Mary	To be honest, right now I don't know what to think - but I'm sure things will become clearer in time. God hasn't let us down yet and although everything looks so bleak and so black ... I think God will have the final word!

Lawyer	You think this episode isn't over yet?

Mary	I know it's not over yet.

Lawyer	Thank you Mary for your courage in coming here today.

(Exit Mary)

Ladies and gentlemen, any mother is going to say her child is special - but what is slightly more unusual about Mary's claim is that she is convinced that Jesus is not just hers, but he's God's son ... yet God - who can do anything - did nothing to save him ...

Let's hear now from someone who witnessed the last moments of Jesus' life. I call upon the Officer of the Guard to take the stand.

(Calls of 'Officer of the Guard'. He enters and takes the witness stand)

I have only a few questions to ask you. Can I begin by asking how long you have performed such morbid duties?

Officer   I have been in the army seven years now and have witnessed over forty crucifixions.

Lawyer   So, you would consider yourself a man of some experience?

Officer   I would.

Lawyer   Did the crucifixion in question go according to plan?

Officer   The crucifixion of Jesus of Nazareth? Yes, it did.

Lawyer   No hiccups?

Officer   No.

Lawyer   Nothing untoward happened?

Officer	Every prisoner deals with the strain of the situation in their own way. Some get angry and shout and protest until they have no breath left. Others are filled with remorse. Others again are just frightened.
Lawyer	And which category did Jesus fall into?
Officer	He didn't really fall into any! Oh, he certainly felt the pain - he couldn't have done anything else! His face was contorted with agony as his hands and feet took the weight of his body ... but there was also an air of sadness about him ... Not sorrow for anything he'd done, but for what others were doing - in fact at one point he shouted out, 'Father, forgive them, for they know not what they do.' Like he wanted God to forgive us!
Lawyer	And you hadn't done anything wrong?
Officer	Exactly!
Lawyer	And he had?
Officer	That's for others to decide. Not me.
Lawyer	Then he died?
Officer	Not before he'd promised one of the crooks hanging beside him that they'd be together soon in heaven.
Lawyer	Jesus told a convicted criminal that they were going to heaven?

Officer	That's right! The man must have been panicking about meeting his maker. They sometimes do when they get near the end. And he turned to Jesus, presumably because Jesus had that 'King of the Jews' notice above his head, and the man said something like, 'Jesus, remember me, when you come into your kingdom.'
Lawyer	And what was Jesus' reply?
Officer	He said that that very day the two of them would be in paradise!
Lawyer	Did anything else happen - or was that the end?
Officer	He shouted out after that. A really loud, chilling cry. I don't speak Aramaic, but I'm told what he shouted was 'My God, my God, why have you forsaken me?' ... I have to admit it unnerved me, it did ...
Lawyer	Unnerved you, why?
Officer	I don't know ... there was just something about it ... something about the whole thing ... in fact, the more I think about it, the more I think he was different.
Lawyer	But it's over now ...
Officer	Almost.

Lawyer	Almost?
Officer	For some reason they wanted a guard over his tomb. I've no idea what they think could happen - that tomb of his has a stone over its entrance that would take at least four people to roll away! Mind you, I wouldn't put it past him!
Lawyer	You didn't seriously think that Jesus could do anything else, did you?
Officer	Let's just say I was happy when that tour of duty was over ...
Lawyer	Thank you officer, you have been most helpful. You may step down.

(Standing, use a podium if possible)

Ladies and gentlemen, we began this week by asking how, in just a few days, the crowds who'd so enthusiastically welcomed Jesus into Jerusalem could so dramatically turn against him. You have been taken through a reconstruction of the events of this, the last week of his life. You have heard from eyewitnesses and listened to their evidence.

I cannot direct you what to think, you have to decide for yourselves, but the following important facts have come to light and need to be borne in mind as you deliberate:

There was an influential group of religious leaders who found Jesus just too difficult to live with, and who were determined to do all they could to get rid of him. They were the ones who offered Judas a good price for selling out his Lord. They were also the ones who knew the places their voices were most likely to be heard. They talked to the crowds, sowed the seeds of dissent and made sure the arm of the Roman government was twisted sufficiently to agree to crucify Jesus. This group can be held primarily responsible for the death of Jesus.

But there were others who are as equally guilty. Pilate, for example, who allowed himself to be so easily swayed for the sake of a bit of peace ... And those so-called 'friends' of Jesus who swore allegiance to him, and then disappeared when he needed them most.

It seems that in this case what people did not do or say played as big a role in the sequence of events as those who were more active and more vociferous ... And the feeling from more than one or two is that this is not where things end.

(Exit Lawyer)

(The service resumes)

Leader   You are requested to stay seated in order to reflect upon what you have heard using the words, 'Jesus, remember me, when you come into your kingdom'. Please sing only every alternate verse.

(Play 'Jesus, Remember Me').

Jesus, remember me ... when you come into your kingdom

Leader   Jesus, remember us ...
As guilty as those crowds so long ago of miscalling you ...
As guilty as your first disciples of staying quiet about
knowing you ...

Jesus, remember me ... when you come into your kingdom

Leader   Jesus, remember us ...
Those who deny and betray you now ... nailing you afresh
to that cross with our silence and inaction.

Jesus, remember me ... when you come into your kingdom

Leader   Jesus, in your love remember us ...
and in your mercy, bring us to where we don't deserve to be
- with you in heaven.

Jesus, remember me ...when you come into your kingdom

(Leader leaves)

Off stage   When evening came ... Joseph of Arimathea took the body
voice   of Jesus and wrapped it in a clean linen shroud and laid it
in his own new tomb that he had hewn in the rock and he
rolled a stone against the door of the tomb ...

(Door slams shut - violently)

It is finished ... isn't it?

*(There is no Benediction and no request for people to leave.
People should get up and leave when they are
ready to do so)*

Holy Week Courtroom Order of Service Summary

Throughout the course of this Holy Week we will invite onto the witness stand some of those who played a part in the events that led up to Easter Sunday. You are asked, as jurors, to listen carefully to the stories being told and to reflect prayerfully upon the evidence given.

The information you will receive is information based on Scripture. There is no law against discussing the details of the case outside these four walls and in fact you are encouraged so to do.

Monday
Remembering how Jesus turned the tables of the moneylenders in the Temple.

Tuesday
Remembering how Jesus allowed a woman to anoint him with expensive perfume.

Wednesday
Remembering the reaction of the Pharisees to Jesus.

Thursday
Remembering the disciples and their relationship to Jesus.

Friday
Remembering Peter's denial, Pilate's complicity, Mary's love and the Roman Officer's belief.

Holy Week - Eyewitness' Monologues

Monday:

Leader
These evenings provide an opportunity for us to make some
time each day to think about the events that led up to the
darkness of Good Friday and to the wonderful glory of
Easter Sunday.

It's not the easiest story to have to listen to - but it's only
when we do listen that the magnitude of what God did
through Jesus begins to hit us -
And we make the marvellous discovery that all he did, he
did with *us* in mind.

Let us pray:

*In the quietness of the evening we pause, Lord Jesus, to think
of the journey you made to the cross
Help us here to walk with you and not to shield our eyes from
all you endured nor close our ears to your anguish and
distress ...
Guide us in your footsteps and fill us afresh with a deep
sense of the full breadth of your loving commitment to every
person in every time ...
Of your willingness to face even death so that we might have
life.
These things we ask in your name and for your sake.
Amen.*

Reading
(from The Message) *Matthew 21:12-17*

Leader	Throughout this week we'll hear eyewitness accounts of some of the things that happened during the last week of Jesus' life.

These eyewitnesses are just ordinary people who saw what they saw and heard what they heard and they've been encouraged simply to sit down and, over a drink, to reflect upon the day drawing to a close.

You are invited to sit with them and to let them talk …

Woman	*(sits at a small table, pours coffee from a pot or flask)*

I was there yesterday - and saw him.

Mind you so did half the city - or more!

The guy has some reputation.

People, even from the farthest, most remote parts of the region have heard of what he can do - which is amazing when you think there's no telephone, no newspapers, no television to help get word round …

… and still *everyone* has heard the stories of his miracle-working.

It meant when we heard he was coming into the city for the Passover we just had to hit the streets to see him for ourselves - if you weren't there then you should have been!

What an atmosphere!

The place was absolutely buzzing! Everyone was chatting away to everyone else - even to complete strangers. They were telling each other what they knew about this teacher down from the hills. To be truthful, I think some of the tales they were telling about his exploits might have grown arms and legs in the telling but everyone swore that what they were saying was Gospel - was true and straight up …

(takes a drink)

By the time he came into sight it was like a carnival and a street party rolled into one! As soon as we saw him coming riding towards us the cheers went up - even although he was just a tiny speck in the distance. Then every palm tree in the district was raided for its branches - and people waved them or if they couldn't get a palm branch they threw their cloaks down on the road. 'Hosanna!' we all shouted at the tops of our voices … 'Hosanna to the Son of David!' - you'd have thought it was the King coming to visit!

But then there was something about him that was right royal … Not his clothes though that's for sure. He was a bit on the scruffy side - like he'd been travelling for weeks in the same stuff!

(takes a drink)

But that was yesterday! Today … well, today is a different story! Today he wasn't the least bit regal - more like a man possessed! He went berserk in the Temple courtyard!

It's true!

I was there! This is hot off the press I'll have you know.

I'd gone along, as you do during Passover, to offer a sacrifice - these guys in the Temple have you over a barrel at this time of year, don't they? Their prices for pigeons and doves are extortionate for the likes of us ordinary folk! And you have to buy them there …

OK. OK. Strictly speaking you don't *have* to buy them there, you can bring your own - but have you ever tried to get a home-grown bird to meet with the approval of the priests? Let's face it, it's not in their interest to have us bypass their traders so the smallest blemish, the tiniest imperfection and your offering is deemed unworthy of sacrifice - you're sent to buy another - so you're just as well taking one of theirs in the first place. And of course, *buying* an offering needs money, doesn't it - and surprise, surprise, the Temple only accepts one coinage - so enter the money changers and lenders who also happen to be employed by the Temple …

(takes a drink)

I know I'm going on about this but, if you'll forgive the pun, it really gets my goat! You've got people there from every part of the country and beyond - all needing to buy birds and animals, and the vast majority of them with non-official currency - can you imagine the profit these guys make? Giving poor exchange rates and charging ludicrously high fees for the privilege! I'm telling you - they have you over a barrel!

Which is why when Jesus started turning over all the tables and chasing those who were manning them, I wasn't exactly upset.

It's true! He turned over their tables! Birds and feathers were flying everywhere! I know I shouldn't have laughed but after the initial shock all I could see was the funny side of it.

You ought to have seen them run - in fact I was surprised at how fast some of them were able to move. You'll know old Benjamin - he's been selling in the Temple since Moses was a boy - the great big round-faced man who can hardly see his toes because his tummy's even rounder - well, even he managed to pick up enough speed to get out of Jesus' way as soon that is - as he saw the whip Jesus held in his hand!

(take a drink)

To be honest, it's the sort of thing lots of people have dreamt of doing but would never actually have done - it was good to see those Temple cheats getting their come-uppance ...

But it makes you wonder how those higher up the ladder will react?

They won't have liked what he did today.

Not one bit.

They tolerated his preaching. They put up with his teaching. They didn't say anything about his miracle-working but this might just be a step too far. We'll have to wait and see.

(takes a drink)

60

Aargh! This coffee's cold! I've been rambling on for ages. It's time I got on with some work. There's a Passover meal to prepare and everyone wants one of Ben Grant's (*or use name of local butcher*) lambs so I'd better get my limbs into gear. I wonder what the rest of the week will bring! I'm telling you, with that Jesus guy around, there's never a dull moment.

(leaves)

Leader   As she goes off to do what housewives do when there's family to feed and things to celebrate, I wonder what the Pharisees were doing ...?

Lamb, I suspect, would be on their minds too - a Lamb to be led to the slaughter.

*(play Lamb of God from Deep Still CD,
see Music Resources section)*

The Temple doors are closed now, for the night. Everyone is sitting in their home - the events of this day already a memory.

The events of tomorrow yet to be revealed.

Go in peace to do what the ordinary people of Jerusalem did that Monday night 2,000 years ago. Eat, talk, work and relax and let tomorrow unfold in its own time.

But unlike those people so long ago, realise how momentous are these events ...

And how selflessly courageous that man from Nazareth was - and is.

(Benediction)   May the blessing of God Almighty ... (etc)

Tuesday:

Leader We stop just for a little while to ponder the last week of
Jesus' life.
Taking a break from the business of our daily routine we set
apart this time to face what he faced.

We need just a little of the courage he showed to help us
begin to understand the awfulness and the beauty of what
he did.

And to realise he did it for us.

Let us pray:

*In quietness we sit before you, our Lord and our God, waiting
to see what this night brings.*
*We come to you in wonder. In awe. Aware of your majesty
and power - and of your selfless gentleness ...*
*We want to meet you, as again you reveal yourself through
your Son.*
*Take this simple time of worship and let your Spirit breath his
life through it so that all that is said and done may be
pleasing in your sight and bring glory to your name.*
For the sake of Jesus Christ our Lord.
Amen

Reading   *(from* The Message*) Luke 19:47-48*

Leader Throughout this week we're hearing eyewitness accounts of
some of the things that happened during the last week of
Jesus' life.
These eyewitnesses are just ordinary people who saw
what they saw and heard what they heard and they've been
encouraged simply to sit down and over a drink, to reflect
upon the day drawing to a close.
You are invited to sit with them and to let them talk ...

| Woman visitor to the Temple | *(sits on a chair at a small table, pours a cup of tea from a pot)* |

I'm one of those strange people who actually *likes* going to the Temple!

I know I can't get into its inner sanctuary because I'm a woman - but it's the atmosphere, the *feel* of the place, it's just so special.

And that's even more true at this time of the year when there are so many people around from so many different backgrounds all gathered together to share in worshipping God ...

I like the chatter. I like the silence ... I even like the sermons! Well, most of them!

(takes a drink)

He was there today.

Jesus, I mean - the young prophet from Nazareth that all the fuss is about. He went down a storm when he first arrived in Jerusalem but he kind of blotted his copybook yesterday by going wild in the Temple. 'My Father's house is a house of prayer!' he bawled, 'and you've turned it into a safe haven for thieves'.

Don't get me wrong - most of the ordinary worshippers who were there thought it was about time someone stood up against our being ripped off in the name of God - but it didn't go down too well with those who run the place ...

When I saw him coming into the Temple again today I did wonder whether they might stop him at the gate - but they didn't. You could see the stall holders hanging onto their tables though as he passed by and one or two of them had a big relative or two standing, arms folded, trying to stare the young teacher out: almost daring him not even to *think* about repeating yesterday's exploits.

He just walked by though.

I followed him - well, as far as I could. You do get a pretty good view from the women's courtyard and you can hear fine - and believe you me, he's worth hearing!

(takes a drink)

Some of those who preach at us are *(looks up)* please forgive me for saying this heavenly Father, but they're *boring*! Dry as dust! Sleep-inducing!

Not him though!

For a start he's younger than most of the ones who get up and speak. In his early 30s I'd say. And he looks ... well, to be honest he looks a bit like those religious hippies who drop out of life - scruffy and unkempt. But see as soon as he opened his mouth ... you couldn't *help* but listen.

Even just his reading of the Scriptures was special - he made them take on a whole new meaning.

And when he taught he didn't come on all heavy like some of them do. He didn't try to prove how clever *he* is and how thick *we* are - or go all holy and preachy. He just spoke.

Quietly.

(takes a drink)

You'd have thought that some of the older folk might have had to strain to hear him - but the place was so quiet that everyone heard, no problem at all, and everyone seemed stunned by the honest simplicity of what he said. By his sincerity.

I say *everyone*, but that's not entirely true. Your ordinary punters certainly did hang on his every word - they, *we*, enjoyed listening to him. Even those you wouldn't normally see anywhere *near* the Temple, those who'd come after the fuss of yesterday just to see what Jesus was going to do today, even they seemed spellbound by his teaching. You could see them thinking 'if only it was like this every week we might come more often!'

But there were others a lot *less* enthusiastic ...

(takes a drink)

Because I'm in the Temple so often I tend to know those who think they run the place - there's nothing better than a bit of people-watching! And I noticed that while Jesus was teaching, they had faces like fizz. You know what I mean by that, don't you?

Faces like thunder! Dark and brooding.

How do I know? Because it was obvious in the way they were *standing* - they looked as though they were having to control their rage with every fibre of their being! No one was listening to *them* and *every*one was listening to this young upstart!

(takes a drink)

Ach! Maybe things'll be different tomorrow and they'll all kiss and make up! Offer Jesus a job at the Temple - there's no surer way of dampening his enthusiasm than by doing that!

Anyway, I've gone on long enough - too long, I know!

It's just that he's such a likeable young man. A bit sad maybe, but so genuine and sincere ... so kindly ...

I'd hate to think what might happen to him if the authorities decide they have to do something about him ...

But then the *people* are behind him and as long as the people are behind him no one will dare do anything - can't have the hordes rebelling now can we!

(takes drink and stands up)

It's time I went to bed! I stood for ages in the queue at Ben Grant's today to order the lamb for Thursday - I'd better get up early tomorrow to make sure I get just the right wine to keep the men happy ...

Not *too* happy of course! Night!

(leaves)

Leader	The people are behind him.
	They're hanging on his every word.
	Yet the clouds darken as the brows of the authorities grow more brooding. Their anger, their resentment poisoning the air.
	The people are behind him ... aren't they?

(play Lamb of God from Deep Still CD)

The temperature drops in the cool Tuesday evening air. Those who'd been in the Temple are home with their families - their minds on other things.

    The disciples think back on another full day - their days are always full since they started to follow Jesus - and wonder what wonderful things might happen tomorrow ...

Jesus ... Jesus is scared.

Go in peace to do whatever this evening holds for you. But every now and then think of how Jesus feels and let his experience of this week touch you and fill you with awe.

(Benediction)   May the blessing of God Almighty ... (etc)

Wednesday:

Leader   The week moves on. Here we are mid-week already,
          Wednesday, and what is really the last oasis of calm before
          the final storm starts to break.

          We stop again: take time out, to think about what happened
          so long ago -
          As if it were happening today.
          And we're helped to do that through the eyes of someone
          who was there ...

          Let us pray:

          Lord Jesus, the week moves on and so does your story.
          You could have stopped it. You could have walked away from
          it all -
          But you didn't. You chose to let others decide your fate: to let
          hate appear to win.
          You elected to go down the path of suffering which is also
          the path of hope.
          Don't let any of us take what you did for granted.
          Don't allow the frequency of the telling of this tale to dull the
          powerful love it portrays -
          Nor make us forget that it was for us you hung and suffered
          there.
          This we ask in your name and for your sake.
          Amen.

Reading   *(from* The Message) *Luke 22:31-34, Matthew 26:35*

67

Leader	Jesus called twelve men in particular to follow him. They became his disciples - and obviously were closest to him throughout the events of this week. We meet one of them tonight. He, like the others we've heard from, has been persuaded to sit down and over a drink to reflect upon the events of this day. You're invited simply to let him talk.
Peter	*(sitting on a bar stool, holding and drinking from a pint of beer)* Following Jesus, once you get into it, is fine! Yes, the initial decision was a big one - it was hard leaving my job and my home (not quite so hard leaving the mother in law …) but once you've made up your mind it's not really that bad! Jesus called me and my brother Andrew one day when we were mending our nets. We're fishermen you understand - or at least we *were* - it's been a long time now though, since we were regularly out on the boat. Must be three years or more! We do still go out from time to time. Well, it's always good to keep your hand in - but this last while things have got so busy we haven't had a chance even to *think* about going fishing. *(takes a drink)* And do you know … I haven't missed it! Not a bit! It's been so amazing to be with Jesus! Lots of people back home said we were nuts to follow him. Said we needed our heads examined. Maybe we do, but how else would we have seen lame people walking, blind people being given their sight, the deaf hearing? Where else would we have heard such wonderful things about God? Making him seem so much closer, so much more real?

Jesus is just great to be around - and far from it being just a phase I'm going through (which is what my mother said my becoming his disciples was) I find I'm enjoying his company more and more. I'd be happy to go *on* following him for ever! In fact, I think I probably will - he needs a good, loyal disciple like me ...

(takes a drink)

He changed my name you know. I haven't always been Peter. My given name is, *was*, Simon. But he said I was to be Peter, meaning the rock.

When I first heard him say that I wasn't too sure what to make of it! I thought, is he taking the mickey out of my size? Saying I'm a bit thick? But then he said rocks are things people use to build on. They give a solid base, a sure foundation - without rock everything falls - and I suddenly thought, I could do a lot worse than be called a rock - I don't think I mind ... 'Peter'... it has a nice ring to it ...

But he totally took the wind out of my sails just a few seconds later when he said, Peter you're the rock ... and I said, yes Lord, and *he* said, upon which I'm going to build my church ...

You could have knocked me down with a feather. Imagine it! Me! Simon Peter! The foundation for Jesus' Church!

Andrew said Jesus must have had too much sun to be saying something as daft - typical little brother!

(takes a drink)

To be honest ... *(pause)* to be honest I think he might be right though. I think maybe Jesus is taking a big risk here ... relying on me.

Oh, don't get me wrong - I'm the most faithful of his faithful followers, no one can top my desire to love and serve him. The others may falter in their faith but *I* never will

It's just that ... well, I'm the sort of person who opens

their mouth and puts their foot right in it! Big style. Oh, is that a new hat you're wearing? It's great! It hides the haircut beautifully ...

No, no, you don't look big in that - not as big as you do in what you were wearing yesterday ...

It's not that I *mean* to be unkind. It just slips out.

(takes a drink)

But then I'm also the sort of person who, when I trust a person, I trust them completely. And I trust Jesus. I trust his judgement - and if he called me a rock then a rock I will be - even if right now I don't feel very secure or very safe ...

He has a knack of managing to see in us what we can't see in ourselves.

Which is why I said what I said.

No matter what the others do, Lord, I will never abandon you. I will never let you down or leave you ...

And I mean it. I won't! I'm a man who stands firm. I'm solid, dependable - the sort of person he can lean on. I'll be there for him, just you wait and see. He won't regret calling me his rock ...

(takes a drink)

It's the Passover tomorrow - as you probably know. We'll be celebrating it with Jesus. We've hired a room - and I hope a cook too because we don't want to be eating the burnt offerings I usually produce!

I suppose I should stop wittering on and go and check that Judas has actually handed over the money so that we can buy the groceries we need. Judas is our treasurer and trying to get money out of him is like trying to get blood out of a stone! He likes to hang on to it and doesn't like to part with it.

Yes, I'd better check he's bought *everything* we need

(gets down off stool)

What would Jesus do without me, eh!

(leaves)

Leader   A Rock Jesus called him.
Solid and dependable he called himself, vowing never to
leave Jesus even if all the others did ... Never.

(play Lamb of God from Deep Still)

The middle of the week; the weekend drawing closer. Only
two more working days and then ...
Then what?

As everyone else plans ahead and starts longing for Friday
night to come, Jesus would rather the clocks stopped and
time stood still.
Looking forward is not something he wants to do - the
thought makes his chest tighten and his breathing quicker.

Not yet! Please not yet!
But the seconds and minutes tick on ...

Go now and think about the time you have ...
However quickly or slowly it passes for you, make the most
of it.
And think of the one who spent his time, making all the time
in the world for you.

(Benediction)   May the blessing of God Almighty ... (etc)

Thursday:

Leader   The Passover has finally arrived. The lengthy preparations have all been leading up to this night. The meal is cooked and families throughout the land are sitting down to share food together - and through that food they celebrate their past as their people have done for centuries.

Tonight though, the past, the present and the future begin to merge as the gates of eternity edge ever wider open.

Let us pray:

In you Lord Jesus, we see all that is powerfully unassuming.
You kept loving and giving even when it met with no thanks.
You were faithful in the teeth of faithlessness.
You were never became bitter at the shallowness of your friends And you willingly walked on: alone, to meet what you knew was to come -
Relying only upon the strength of your Father.
May we follow your footsteps; hear your voice and sense something of how you felt so that we might understand more fully what you did -
and appreciate why you did it.
This we ask in your name and for your sake.
Amen.

Reading   *(from* The Message*) Luke 22:7-13*

Leader   This has the feel of a long night about it.
Most family celebrations do in one way or another!
Sit back and listen as the owner of the upper room puts his feet up and over a glass, reflects on those he's let the room to …

Landlord   *(at a table with a glass of wine and some torn bread, as if left over)*

Ahh! This is the best part of a long day. Sitting down in the peace and quiet of the evening once everyone's gone- glass in hand ...

(pause as he takes a drink)

We'd that chap in here tonight. The fellow from Nazareth. You know the one I mean, don't you? - he's got twelve disciples and came bursting into Jerusalem in a blaze of glory riding on a donkey.

He wasn't how I imagined him to be at all. Much quieter. Nowhere near as pushy - in fact quite unassuming ...

(takes a drink)

Those friends of his are some bunch! What a mix! Rough and ready fishermen to a learned doctor and all shades in between. Good guys though - only one of them rubbed me up the wrong way. The purse-keeper. Wasn't exactly overly-keen to pay the bill for the room and the food ... In fact he left early. Didn't seem to want to stay to the end ...

We do this every year, you know. Let out a room and cook for visitors come to the city for the Passover celebrations. It's a great way of meeting new people and since we have no family of our own, it's good to have the company. And this lot were easy to look after. The usual bread, and one of those famous Ben Grant's lambs done to perfection with herbs and spices - and of course some bread to mop up the gravy ... all part of the tradition of this night.

(takes a drink)

I tell you what was different though. They didn't have the youngest or the most junior member of their party washing the feet of the others - it was Jesus, the Teacher, who did it!

73

To be honest, I don't think anyone else *wanted* to do something as menial. I think there was a bit of tension there. So Jesus just got up and left the room and came back with a towel wrapped round his waist and a basin of water and he went round each of them - which had a far better effect than if he'd lectured them about how they should be helping each other!

You should have seen their faces! You could have heard a pin drop the place went so quiet!

Well, at least until Jesus reached the big fisherman, what was his name ...? Peter - yes, Peter. Peter started to make a fuss - no, Lord, you can't wash my feet, no, please don't. But the Teacher told him, if I don't wash your feet then you can't be a part of me. Then wash not only my feet but *all* of me, Peter said - that brought a smile to Jesus' face! Over the top as usual, Peter, he said, I'll just do your feet.

(takes a drink)

Everything else went pretty much as usual. There were the normal prayers and whatnot that accompany the meal - and everyone chatted away and seemed to have a fine old time.

I stayed in the room while they ate, just in case they needed anything. So that I could fetch it. But as I say they were easy to please and happy with what they got.

I did notice one thing which was a bit different.

I don't know if it's because they're from Nazareth and it's something folks in Nazareth do, but they did one thing we city Jews don't do. They had an extra 'bit' to the evening's proceedings. At the end of the meal the Teacher tore apart some bread and he raised a glass of wine and he shared both the bread and the wine - in the one glass - around the room ... I've never seen that done before.

I remember he said something about this being his body broken and his blood spilled and a way of remembering him ... I remember because for some reason when he said that it sent a shiver down my spine - even now it spooks me a bit.

(takes a drink)

Anyway! They all seemed to enjoy their evening - although, as I say, the money man left early. The rest of them though, left quite late and left together. I asked if they were turning in and although the disciples said yes, they probably would because they were tired, Jesus suggested they go to the garden - the one they call Gethsemane - just for a little while and so they all left to go there.

That must be about an hour maybe two hours ago now. I think they thought they might get some peace out there but I heard what sounded like an army heading over that way just a little while ago. I just happened to go out for a bit of fresh air when they all passed, armed to the hilt. Looks like they're expecting trouble.

I hope the Teacher and his friends don't get caught up in the middle of it ...

(gets down and yawn and stretch)

Wine is nice to drink but it doesn't half make you sleepy! I'm told that in its more vinegary form it acts as a painkiller - at least so the mother-in-law says - so it must be true!

Well, that's it. All the excitement over for another year. Time to make for bed and to dream sweet dreams ... Night.

(leaves)

Leader   They wait now in the garden ... and no doubt as they do so, before their eyes grow too heavy, they mull over their evening together.

They were used to Jesus saying and doing strange things but tonight they'd witnessed the strangest yet.
'In the course of their meal, having taken and blessed the bread, he broke it and gave it to them. Then he said, Take, this is my body.

Taking the chalice, he gave it to them, thanking God, and they all drank from it. He said, This is my blood, God's new covenant, poured out for many people.'

All there ate and drank. *All* of them.

> *(Play Lamb of God from Deep Still CD. Hand out bread, wait, then pour wine and pass round ...)*

Leader   Stomachs full, eyes heavy, the disciples slept while Jesus in utter anguish spoke to his Father.

Go now, aware that others have concerns we know nothing about.
And go aware that Jesus is on his knees, pouring out his heart, tears streaming down his face -
As he prepares himself for what he knows is soon, so soon, to come.

(Benediction) May the blessing of God Almighty ... (etc)

Good Friday:

(NB - this service is longer than the others and may be more appropriately held in the evening)

Hymn	*When I survey the wondrous cross* *(CH3 254)*

Leader
: Let us pray:
Lord Jesus Christ, we cannot even begin to understand why you should have done what you did -
we are filled with shame that you should have had to and with awe that you should want to -
your unselfish love and courage goes beyond anything we have ever seen or known.
We are grateful though, that you did face that terrible cross, and that you did it bearing each one of us in mind.
Open our hearts to you this night, Lord, and open our lives to your Spirit...
give us the courage to acknowledge what you did - and our part in it
these prayers we offer in your own name and for your sake, Amen

Peter
: I had no idea things could ever get this bad!
I can't lift my head to look at anyone. I'm so ashamed.
I want to run and hide in the shadows - or walk into the sea and be done with it! I can't believe what they've done to him
…
And I can't believe I let them …

(*blows nose*) I'll stand by you. I'll never leave you. You can count on me - I said all those things to him and meant them. At least I *thought* I did - but when they came for him … I ran.

I ran and ran and ran as fast as I could. Big brave Peter … not!
I can't believe it!

We'd had a wonderful Passover celebration - the twelve of us plus Jesus. The food was great, the room was cosy - only Judas was out of sorts and now I can see why! *(angry)*

How could he have done such a thing? Our own Judas! How could he? And with a kiss? What had Jesus ever done to deserve that! Even just the thought of it turns my stomach. What *made* him do it?

(exasperated) But then the rest of us are just as bad. We betrayed him too. Not for money. But we betrayed him by running out on him.

They took him when we were in the garden. It was only him they wanted - but just in case they decided to take us too, we all made our escape in as many different directions as we could as fast as we could.

So here I am. Trying as best I can to see where they're taking him - but from a safe distance.
I *want* to get closer. I want to shout his name - hear *him* speak mine; see *him* look at me just one more time ... but my fear won't let me.
I am *so* scared. A big grown man like me. Scared for me ... *and* for him.

Woman	*(coming towards Peter)* Aren't you one of them? *(Peter turns his back on her.)* You! Hey big guy - you were with him, weren't you?
Peter	Me? With who? With that preacher from Nazareth - you must be joking!
Woman	You were! You even talk like him! You have the same accent. You're one of his followers, aren't you?

| Peter | Look, I'm telling you - I've never set eyes on the man before, let alone followed him anywhere! Now leave me alone! |

| Woman | Ooooh touchy! But listen, I *never* forget a face and no matter how strongly you try to deny it, I know you were with him. I saw you! With my own eyes! You and him together! Admit it! |

| Peter | I admit nothing! I swear to God I have never met the man in my life - would never *want* to meet him. Get off my case woman, and you and your imaginings get back to work before I tell your boss how much you're annoying his customers! |

(Woman exits as cock crows ... Peter buries his head in his hands, leaves during hymn as Carpenter enters)

| Hymn | *O Sacred Head, sore wounded (CH3 253)* |

| Carpenter | *(takes a mug of tea)* |

These hands of mine *(look at them)* shape wood. They cut down trees and carve out bowls and create the tables to set them on.

(drinks)

They're good too at what they do, these hands of mine. *(turn them over)* They can smooth down even the toughest knot ... I've made cribs for babies, dressers for ladies, carts and stools - I've even made a boat - but just for my own use. Not much call for boats here in the city.

79

And I make crosses. They're not exactly hard to put together - you don't need anything too fine, just something rough and ready. And they provide a steady, easy income for a carpenter … I made three of them. For today I mean.

(pauses to drink)

His hands must look a lot like mine. *(look at hands again)* Usually they tell me what those who are to die have done - the soldiers tell me when I go with the crosses - but I'm not sure what exactly his crime is. To be honest I'm not sure *anyone* knows for certain - it seems they just want him out the way.
Well out of the way.
And for me it's normally just a job. *(shrug)* Something that has to be done. Tonight though …
Tonight I can't get him out of my head.
I know there are three, but it's the carpenter, like me, I keep thinking of.

(pauses to drink)

They'd bruised him.
They'd whipped him until he bled. It's what they always do - but the soldiers made a special crown for him - a crown of thorns which they put on his head - *forced* it on, of course, so that the thorns dug in.
Then the cross these hands made, he carried.

(drinks again)

I always follow on - in case there are any minor adjustments that have to be done. And tonight, as usual, I made my way with them to Golgotha.
The weight was almost too much for him.
The beating had weakened him, sapped his strength.
I don't know why, perhaps because they were scared their star attraction would die before he got to the hill outside the

80

city, but the soldiers detailed to get the three of them there, got an onlooker to carry his cross for him.
And on we went.

(drinks)

The hill was as crowded as I've ever seen it. The crosses were laid down and the three men were nailed to them. With the first hammer blow the noisy crowds who'd been screaming for blood suddenly fell silent - and silent they remained until the crosses were hoisted into position.
Then ... then they cheered.

That's about as much as I could take.
My eyes never left his face during that time - and his eyes never left mine.
I've seen lots of crucifixions - but I couldn't watch that one.
So I came home.
And here I am.
Drinking tea and feeling numb.
Oh, *so* numb.
And strangely cold. *(he shivers. Exits during hymn as Official enters)*

Hymn   *There is a green hill far away (CH3 241)*

Official   *(carrying hip flask)*

Some cheek that!

You'll never believe this but that guy up there on the middle cross, the one with the sign above his head saying 'King of the Jews' - he's just this minute told the thieving wretch on his left that God's waiting for him.

Waiting for *him*! For that convicted sneak-thief ready to steal whatever he could lay his hands on! What kind of God is going to welcome *him*?

81

And what *right* has that Nazarene, I'm not going to soil my lips by saying his name, what right has he even to *think* of suggesting what God will and will not do!

'Jesus remember me, when you come into your kingdom' - that's what the whimpering wretch said, and he said, 'It's okay mate, today *you* are going to be with me in heaven.'

In heaven!

Good grief! What on earth is this world coming to that common criminals think they can hand out places in heaven!

(drinks and stomps off as Mary enters)

(play CD Lamb of God from Deep Still)

Mary   *(distraught, carrying nothing)*

I stand and watch as life ebbs from him.

My boy.

The one God had given me to carry and nurse and watch grow and mature.

I'm trying to stay strong for him. I don't want to add to his anguish.

But I can't help but cry.

My heart is breaking tonight. Breaking into hundreds, no *thousands* of pieces. Shattering ... And it doesn't feel as though it will ever go back together again.

I can't think of a more cruel way to die.

Or of a more painful way.

And yet even as he hangs there he's thinking of me.

He's thinking of *me*!

He's asked John to take his place - to look after me, as his own mother - woman, behold thy son, he said, and son, behold thy mother ...

As if *he* ever could be replaced.

This is the hardest thing I have ever done, standing here, watching and waiting for the end.
Oh how I pray it will come quickly! Please, Father, take him to you ... take him home ... take him soon.

My boy.

They offer him vinegar.
He refuses it and cries out - the scream tearing my very soul apart - my God, my God, why have you forsaken me?
I can't take any more and just as I think I will have to run, the sky darkens.

I look up and his head drops.
He's gone.
I can hold back no longer. My screams pierce the air.
No!

(Mary cries and sobs, remaining in an attitude of grief)

(Prayer as 'Jesus remember me' is sung. Please sing, then pause for prayer, then sing again ...)

Leader	Jesus remember me ...
All	Jesus, remember us ...
Leader	As guilty as those crowds so long ago, of miscalling you ... As guilty as your first disciples of staying quiet about knowing you ...
	Jesus, remember me ...
All	Jesus, remember us ...

Leader   Those who deny and betray you now ... nailing you afresh
          to that cross with our silence and inaction.

          Jesus, remember me ...

          Jesus, in your love remember us ...
          And in your mercy, bring us to where we don't deserve to be
          - with you in heaven.

          Jesus, remember me ...

                         (switch off all lights)

Single   *(speaking through the darkness)*
voice only
          When evening came ... Joseph of Arimathea took the body
          of Jesus and wrapped it in a clean linen shroud and laid it
          in his own new tomb which he had hewn in the rock and he
          rolled a stone against the door of the tomb ...

          It is finished ... is it?

                   *(Please note there should be no Benediction. The
                   congregation is asked to leave in their own time).*

Holy Week Monologues Order of Service Summary

Throughout the course of this Holy Week we will listen to eye witness accounts from some of those who observed the events that led up to Easter Sunday. You are asked to listen carefully to the stories being told and to reflect prayerfully upon the attitudes and characters revealed.

The information you will receive is based on Scripture. Please discuss the stories and the tellers, thinking about life at the time and how the people involved are not much different from us today.

Monday
A simple woman reflects on Jesus - how he came into Jerusalem in a blaze of glory, and then turned over the moneylenders' tables in the Temple

Tuesday
The Temple visitor - a woman who likes spending time there reflects on the day after the rumpus with the moneylenders

Wednesday
Peter reflects on his life with Jesus, how it changed and how much he now enjoys it…

Thursday
The Landlord of the Upper Room reflects on Jesus and the Last Supper with his disciples

Friday
Remembering Peter - his agony at denying Jesus, the Carpenter who built the cross, an Official furious to defend the justice system and Jesus' mother Mary, having watched him die.

Easter Sunday Dawn Service

Leader   They thought they'd killed him.
They thought they'd got rid of the one who challenged and surprised them.
They assumed he was dead - and buried.
Safely entombed, wrapped in his shroud.

But on this day, just as the sun was rising, they discovered that not even death could hold him.
The tomb was empty - Jesus was alive!
He had risen!

And today we meet …
… just as the sun is rising discovering afresh that death does not have the final say.
We too shout Hallelujah - because -

Christ has died.
Christ is risen.
Christ will come again.

*(Scene: Mary in the garden near to the tomb
where Jesus was laid.)*

Leader   Let's hear from Mary - the first to arrive at the tomb.

Mary   I hadn't slept all night - neither had any of the others. I couldn't wait until the Sabbath was over. At the first hint of morning I made my way to the tomb. Why? Because I wanted to do what we didn't have time to do on Friday - I wanted to spend time with him. Quietly. Privately. So I left the others dozing and sneaked out. The streets were empty. My mind, though, was full - full of all the things I wished I'd said, I wished I'd done …

I was at the tomb almost before I knew it and there I found ... Well, I found ... I found it empty! The enormous stone that had been over its entrance was rolled away. I couldn't believe it! And I didn't dare look in! Instead, I ran back to fetch Peter and John and they came tearing down to see what I was talking about ...

And when they got to the tomb, they went in. They saw the linen wraps which had covered his body just lying there - but there was no body in sight! They went back home - I stayed and cried. Yes, I cried my eyes out. It was the final straw as far as I was concerned. They'd taken him. Stolen him and left us not knowing ...

Then someone whom I thought was the gardener appeared. I asked him, pleaded with him, to tell me where they'd taken him and all he said was ... 'Mary' and I realised ... it was him! Jesus! Alive! And I ran off, as he told me to, to tell the others!

Leader	Let us pray:

Lord Jesus Christ,
We greet you this Easter morning as our risen Lord.
Open our eyes to see you around us and within us and send us from here filled with joy and excitement at the Good News that you are alive and with us for ever more.

Song	*Jubilate, everybody (SOGP 59)*

Leader	With the dawning of each new day we are offered the chance of a fresh start. With the dawning of each new day we are encouraged to build on, or to move on from, the past. With the dawning of each new day, we are invited to try our best to make the most of what lies ahead and to live life to the full - and that's especially true on this Easter day.

But Easter goes further than that.
Easter reminds us that we start each and every day, not alone, but with our risen and living Lord by our side.
It reminds us that the God who came to us at Christmas, has promised never to leave us ...
And it encourages us to hold on to this promise of help and strength, of hope and joy for this and every day, for now and always ...

And these are not empty words. They are promises made by God and kept by God - that's why we are encouraged with all his people everywhere, on this morning of mornings, to shout Hallelujah! from the tops of our voices. He is risen! He's alive! And he is with us for ever more. Hallelujah!

This surely, is Good News which is worth sharing - worth passing on ... turn to your neighbours and greet them with the words, Peace be with you, Hallelujah!

Song   *(round):Allelu, allelu, allelu, allelujah*
                                  Praise ye the Lord

Leader   *God's promise to us is that his love and mercy shall last for ever, as fresh as the morning, as sure as the sunrise.*

                May God bless us this Easter Day;
                may he fill us with the joy of the resurrection
                and send us from here,
                our hearts filled with the love and peace of the risen Christ
                and ready to love and serve him daily.

                And may the blessing of God Almighty; Father, Son and Holy Spirit, be with you all now and for ever more.
                Amen.

Easter Sunday Evening Emmaus Service

Hymn   *This joyful Eastertide (CH3 271)*

Leader   Let us pray:

               Lord Jesus Christ, you meet us;
               your hands still holed
               but your breath warm
               and your conversation engaging.
               Death has not changed your accent
               or diminished your love.

               And though the world
               still shows signs of its imperfection,
               the good news is that you have destined it
               and all its people
               to be made whole.

               So, as on this Easter evening
               we are gathered in your house,
               cheered by the Gospel,
               join us
               as you joined your first disciples
               and make our worship here
               your Emmaus road.

Song   *Our Lord Christ hath risen ... (SOGP 91)*

          (Scene: Two disciples walking in from the doors to the
                     centre of the service.)

Disciple One   What a day!

Cleopas   What a week!

Disciple One	One we'll never forget!
Cleopas	I certainly won't!
Disciple One	At the time though, it just didn't make any sense. None at all.
Cleopas	I can remember feeling sick - physically sick.
Disciple One	And light headed ...
Cleopas	Why? That's what I couldn't get my head round ... Why did he have to die?
Disciple One	And in such a way!
Cleopas	We talked a lot - didn't we - on the way home?
Disciple One	We could probably have taken the world record in talking! We went over and over and over everything ...
Cleopas	And went over it and over it and over it again!
Disciple One	That wonderful entry into Jerusalem, with everyone shouting and cheering ...

Cleopas	And those more chilling cheers just a few days later of 'Crucify him! Crucify him!'
Disciple One	We felt so desperate when they sentenced him.
Cleopas	So lost ... We thought, I mean really thought, he was special, that he had a purpose and a mission - and it was all snuffed out so quickly.
Disciple One	Like a candle in a draught!
Cleopas	Very poetic!
Disciple One	But true too. It was as though with his final cry on the cross all our hopes and dreams had been shattered ...
Cleopas	Remember how dark everything went. It was as if the very heart of the entire world had been broken.
Disciple One	God's heart ...
Cleopas	We talked a lot about that too as we walked. About where God was, why he'd let this happen.
Disciple One	It was just beyond us - and the more we talked the more confused and upset we became.
Cleopas	We didn't notice him, did we ... coming up to us?

Disciple One	One minute there was just the two of us - the next this stranger was with us.
Cleopas	And he joined in our conversation.
Disciple One	He asked what it was we were discussing so earnestly.
Cleopas	He didn't seem to know what had happened - he must have been about the only one who didn't - so I told him!
Disciple One	And then he began to open up the Scriptures to us, showing us where God had warned of these things happening.
Cleopas	He lifted the darkness hanging over us, didn't he?
Disciple One	Things didn't seem quite as hopeless when he talked.
Cleopas	And then we arrived home - and he made to go on
Disciple One	But we persuaded him to stay and eat with us.
Cleopas	We hadn't realised how hungry we were until that point - with all the fuss and turmoil we hadn't eaten all day - and he seemed hungry too - at least he agreed readily enough to join us.
Disciple One	So we sat at the table.

Cleopas	And we asked him to say grace.
Disciple One	And he took bread and broke it and blessed it.
Cleopas	And we finally realised it was him! Jesus!
Disciple One	He was alive!
Cleopas	Then he disappeared!
Disciple One	But we'd seen him and couldn't wait to tell the others.
Cleopas	Without stopping for breath we grabbed our coats and virtually ran back to Jerusalem!
Disciple One	The tiredness had gone - we were so excited!
Cleopas	So happy!
Disciple One	So relieved!
Cleopas	What wonderful news we had to tell the others!
Disciple One	We couldn't wait to pass it on!

Cleopas	Even now it makes me want to run and jump - and even dance!
Disciple One	Now, now, Cleopas, remember your zimmer!
Hymn	*Come risen Lord (CH3 572)*

The Communion

Leader	After the terrible events of Good Friday and the days that followed, two of Jesus' followers, as we heard, made their way from Jerusalem to their home town of Emmaus. On the way they were joined by a stranger who talked to them and calmed them - long before they fully realised who he was.

A reminder to us all, that Christ comes alongside us - sometimes uninvited, often unrecognised - but always when we need him most - and he walks with us sympathetically ... and helpfully ...

It was when the two travellers shared a simple meal with the stranger, that all became clear - so let us now do likewise and invite the one who is walking with each one of us to come and stay with us so that, as we share the bread and the wine, we too might have our eyes opened and feel our heart burning within us.

You who are with friend and stranger, with young and old, come join us at this table ... Come close to us that we may come close to you ... forgive us that we may forgive one another ... and renew us so that where we have failed, we may begin again. Amen.

Invitation

Leader   At the Last Supper, Jesus, sharing bread and wine, invited
the disciples to walk in his footsteps and to share his journey.
He walked with two more disciples as they tried to
understand Easter and revealed himself when he sat down to
eat with them ... Here, tonight, through this bread and wine
we too are invited to make an Easter journey with Christ.
Here, tonight, through bread and wine, we too are
encouraged to take our place among all Jesus' disciples in
every time and place, united as his body ... therefore as a
sign of our willingness to journey with him, can I invite you
to come and stand together around this his table, come and
taste of this bread and wine, bought at such great price, gifts
of the earth, but food both of earth and heaven.

The Narrative

Among friends, gathered round a table as we are tonight,
Jesus took bread and, having blessed it, he broke the bread
and gave it to his disciples saying, 'This is my body. It is
broken for you. Do this to remember me.'

In the same way he took wine and, having given thanks
for it, he poured it out and gave the cup to the disciples
saying, 'This cup is our new relationship with God, sealed
with my blood. Drink from it all of you, to remember me.'

So now, following Jesus' example, we take this bread and
this wine - the ordinary things of the world - through which
God will bless us. And as Jesus offered thanks, so do we.

Let us pray:

Lord Jesus Christ, present with us now,
as we do in this place what you did in an upstairs room and
in that house in Emmaus; breathe your Spirit upon us and
upon this bread and wine, that they may be heaven's food
and drink for us - renewing, sustaining and making us whole
- and that we may be your body on earth, continuing your
selfless love and care in the world.

(Take and break bread)
When Jesus was among his friends, gathered round a table, he took bread, broke it, and said, 'This is my body. It is broken for you. Do this to remember me.'

(Take cup)
And in the same way, he took a cup of wine and said, 'This is the new relationship with God, made possible because of my death. Drink from it, all of you, to remember me.'

We do now, what Christ himself has asked us to do. Knowing that it's here, through these simple things, that we, like so many before us, can discover the wonderful truth that our Lord has indeed risen and is with us for ever.

Look, look, here is your risen Lord coming to you in bread and wine … these are the gifts of God for his people … taste and see that the Lord is good.
(Share the communion)

(After communion)
As this broken bread was scattered through fields and hills before being gathered to become one, so may we and everyone else be gathered from the ends of the earth into Christ's kingdom.

Let's pray:

Lord Jesus Christ you have put your life in our hands, now we put our lives in yours.
Take us.
Shake us.
Remake us.
What we have been is no longer important.
It is what, with you, we can be.
Starting now.
Help us to be your Easter people, living in hope, here, and wherever we may be.
Amen.

Hymn	*How great Thou art ... (SOGP 86)*

Leader   Tonight we've gone through again the story of the two
disciples walking home to Emmaus - now we come to the bit
of the tale I like best - if you've been here before you'll know
what I'm talking about ...

My favourite bit is not actually in the story as we read it -
but it is there if you use a little imagination and read
between the lines. `To my mind, with what happened that
night there's as much that's important left unsaid as there is
spoken.

Remember the disciples had walked home from
Jerusalem slowly because they were exhausted after all that
had happened. Remember how hungry they'd been - so
hungry that they pressed the stranger who'd been walking
with them into joining them for some supper ...? How much
of that supper do you think they ate?

My guess is, not a lot.

It was when Jesus blessed their food that the two
recognised him and we're told that as soon as they did,
Jesus vanished, and the two disciples upped sticks and
headed straight back to Jerusalem - in fact the impression
given is that they virtually raced back to the other disciples,
no longer the least bit tired.

Now, I know I have an over-active imagination, but when
I read that tale, the picture that immediately springs to my
mind is one in which the two disciples, keen to get back to
the others as fast as they possibly can, grab some of the
bread from the table, maybe a wineskin too, stuff these
things into their pockets and head out the door, ready to
munch as they go. (Meals without wheels I suppose!)

It's the bread being stuffed into the pockets that I like
best.

And I like it best because it shows how excited they were
... and it means they took something tangible from this
encounter with Jesus away with them.

Like those two disciples, tonight and over the Easter
period, I hope we've had the chance to meet in unexpected

ways with the risen Lord. In the Lent Study Groups, in the Holy Week prayers there have been this past week, in the Good Friday service, the dawn service, this morning's service and tonight as we've shared the bread and the wine together ...

My hope is that we too have managed to grab whatever morsels of food for thought we can from all these things, to tuck away in our pockets to keep us going on our journey through the next few days, weeks, months ... a journey we look upon as more exciting now and more breathtaking because we've encountered the living Lord who's blown the cobwebs away.

Let's give thanks now for all Easter stands for - and ask for the courage to make every day an Easter day - one in which we walk with and talk with the living Lord who walks with us always into whatever comes our way.

Can I ask you to turn to your neighbour and to tell them just one thing about this Easter you'll remember ...

We offer all our conversations to God and give him thanks for all the bread he's given us to fill the pockets of our faith.

Hymn   *To God be the glory! (CH3 374)*

Benediction

Advent Adventures

by Susan M Brown

"Have you heard the latest? We're doing an Advent play!"

- "What, with tea towels over the head, and dressing gowns and all the rest?"

"No! A bit more up-to-date than that…"

How did Rolf Harris and a talking donkey get involved in the Advent story? Who will be the last to be voted out of the Big Brother Stable? And what do the Archers and the Flintstones have to tell us about Christmas? Advent Adventures supplies the answer! This book offers a series of short, quirky dramas filled with Susan Brown's appealingly off-the-wall humour; these sketches can be put on in Advent services, at school, or anywhere else - all the world's a stage!

Susan Brown wrote these dramas for her own community to use. Tried and tested material, which can easily be put on by young people and adults alike, and watched with enjoyment by all - these sketches will appeal to everyone.

£7.99, ISBN 1904325122, available from Booksource 08702402182 and all good Christian Retailers.

Simple sketches for the Advent Season

Advent Adventures

PHOTOCOPIABLE

By Susan M Brown

The Widening Road:

from Bethlehem to Emmaus

Exploring the Gospel of Luke

Leith Fisher

The Gospel of Luke is one of the treasures of the Christian church. Artful and engaging in his narrative style, Luke has the wonderful capacity to surprise his readers, to tell stories with a devastating twist in the tale, or to show a sudden new vista on reality. Luke's gospel has also exerted a massive influence on the way we see our world. Phrases and images from Luke have been part and parcel of our culture for centuries, and some of Luke's basic themes have shaped both faith and culture enormously.

Leith Fisher shows us an accessible way to engage with this gospel and opens up Luke's vivid picture-gallery of stories to all readers: read on to learn more of the road which beckons in this most universal of the gospels. Suitable for personal or for group reading, this book divides the gospel account into manageable parts so that it can be read altogether, or over a period of study. It could form the basis for a year's preaching through Luke or for a series of group studies; its forty sections also make it suitable for the days of Lent.

£11.99, ISBN 1904325114, available from Booksource 08702402182 and all good Christian Retailers.

the widening road:

from Bethlehem to Emmaus

Exploring the Gospel of Luke
Leith Fisher